# Armor and helmets

## Helmets

Helmets protected part or all of the head and face in battle and sometimes the neck too. They were made in many different shapes over the ages.

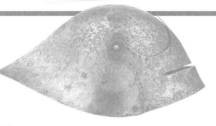

### SALLET
A dish-like helmet was used in the 1450s. It had a leather lining and was often worn with a bevor, a metal plate protecting the lower face and throat.

### MAIL COIF
The mail hood was fitted with a flap called a ventail, which protected the chin. It was worn under a conical or basin-type helmet.

### BARBUTE
This one-piece helmet looks rather like a helmet from ancient Greece, but it was worn from the 1350s to the 1450s.

### NASAL HELMET
The conical helmet had a bar called a "nasal" to protect the nose. It was worn by the Normans in the 1000s and 1100s.

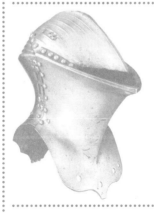

### FROG-MOUTH HELM
The great helm was a bucket-like helmet covering the whole head and neck. This version with a front like a frog's mouth was popular from the 1390s.

### BASCINET
This was a basic helmet with added neck protection and a visor. Sometimes, the visor was pointed like a snout to deflect a blow from a weapon.

### CLOSE HELMET
This type of helmet from the 1500s included a protective bevor and visor and was often topped with a feather plume.

## My Findout facts:

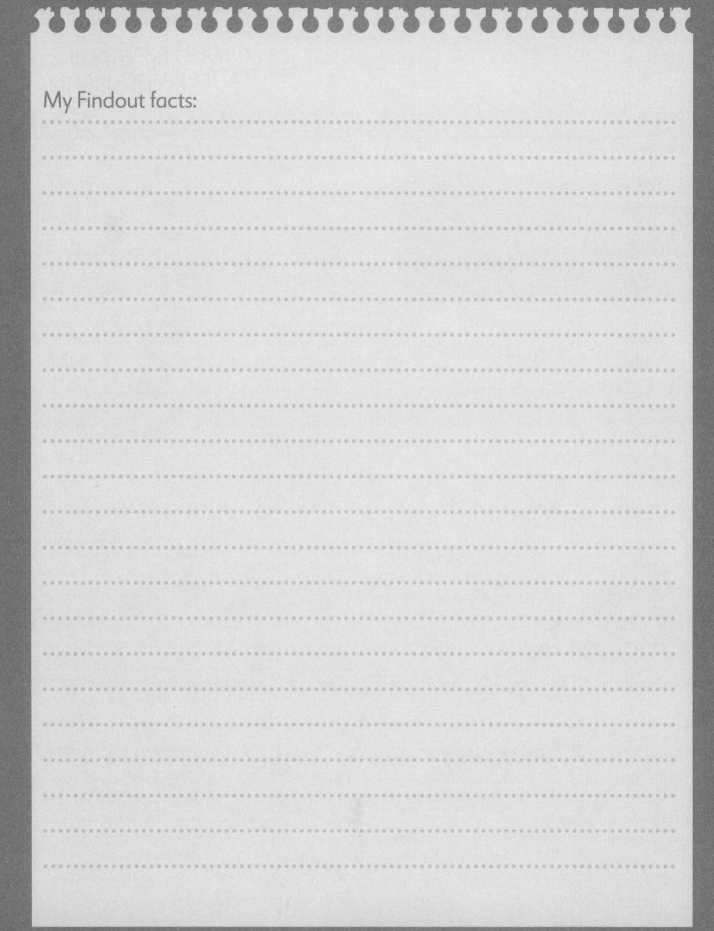

# DK findout!
# Castles

Author: Philip Steele
Consultant: Dr. Jenny Benham

**Senior editor** Satu Hämeenaho-Fox
**Assistant editors** Shambhavi Thatte, Andrew Korah
**Senior art editors** Ann Cannings, Nidhi Mehra
**Project art editors** Nehal Verma, Emma Hobson
**US Senior editor** Allison Singer
**Americanizer** Christopher Stolle
**DTP designers** Jagtar Singh, Sachin Gupta
**Picture researcher** Sakshi Saluja
**Jacket coordinator** Francesca Young
**Jacket designer** Dheeraj Arora
**Managing editors** Laura Gilbert, Alka Thakur Hazarika
**Managing art editors** Diane Peyton Jones, Romi Chakraborty
**Delhi team head** Malavika Talukder
**Pre-production producer** Heather Blagden
**Producer** John Casey
**Creative director** Helen Senior
**Publishing director** Sarah Larter
**Educational consultant** Jenny Lane-Smith

First American Edition, 2019
Published in the United States by DK Publishing
1450 Broadway, 8th Floor, New York, New York 10018

Copyright © 2019 Dorling Kindersley Limited
DK, a Division of Penguin Random House LLC
19 20 21 22 23  10 9 8 7 6 5 4 3 2 1
001–311569–June/2019

Published in Great Britain by Dorling Kindersley Limited

A catalog record for this book
is available from the Library of Congress.
ISBN: 978-1-4654-8153-5 (Flexibound)
978-1-4654-8154-2 (Hardcover)

Printed and bound in China

A WORLD OF IDEAS:
SEE ALL THERE IS TO KNOW

www.dk.com

# Contents

Lute

Heraldic shield

Dagger

Peregrine
falcon

Farmer

Château de Gisors

# What is a castle?

Rulers built castles between about 1,100 and 500 years ago in Europe and parts of Asia. Their massive stone towers loomed over places from valleys to seashores. Castles were built for defense but were also home to many people.

Bodiam Castle, East Sussex, UK

### Regional power

A castle was a power base. It could be used to guard a route, to prevent an invasion, or to keep control over a rebellious region of the country.

### Administration

Castles could be used to rule in ways that weren't military. Taxes were stored, law cases were heard, and meetings were held in castles. Some were part of a town.

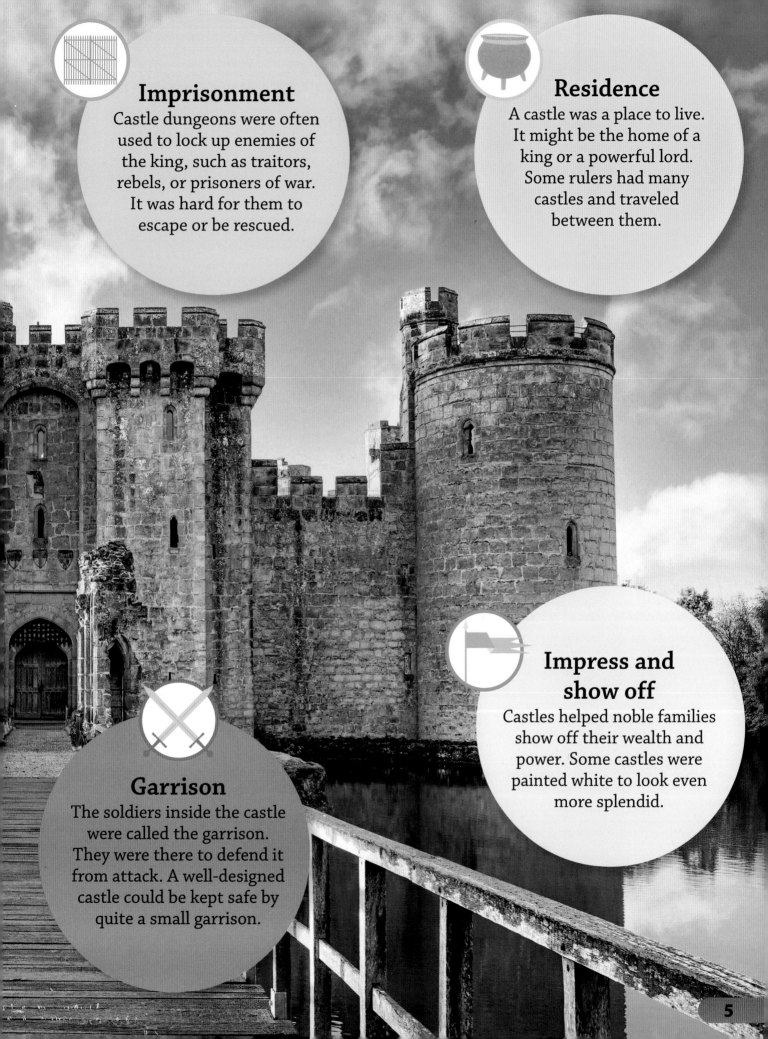

## Imprisonment

Castle dungeons were often used to lock up enemies of the king, such as traitors, rebels, or prisoners of war. It was hard for them to escape or be rescued.

## Residence

A castle was a place to live. It might be the home of a king or a powerful lord. Some rulers had many castles and traveled between them.

## Garrison

The soldiers inside the castle were called the garrison. They were there to defend it from attack. A well-designed castle could be kept safe by quite a small garrison.

## Impress and show off

Castles helped noble families show off their wealth and power. Some castles were painted white to look even more splendid.

# Wooden castles

The Normans began building castles with timber in the 9th century BCE. This castle design is called "motte and bailey." The first "keeps," or towers, stood on top of a mound called a motte. Below the motte was an open area called a bailey. The whole site was protected by fences and ditches.

## Bailey
The bailey was an enclosed flat area with a hall, an armory, workshops, and stables and sheds for animals.

## Palisade
Palisades are defensive fences or walls made from wood. They surrounded the motte, the bailey, and the keep.

## Moat
A ditch around the castle could be filled with water but was often dry and filled with pointed stakes. This made it harder for armies to attack the outer wall.

## Drawbridge
Bridges across the ditches could be raised when the castle was under attack.

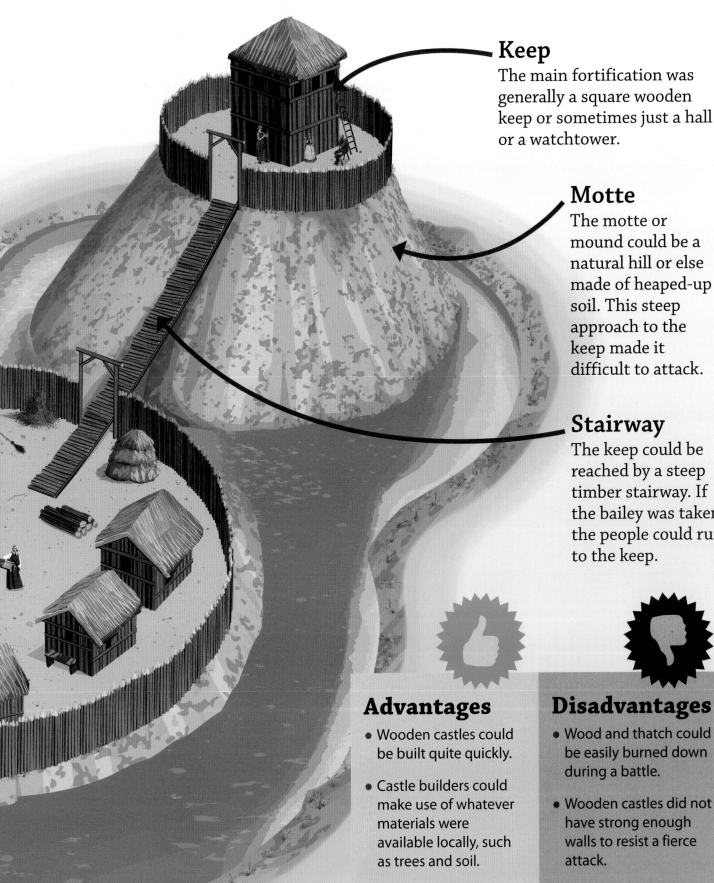

## Keep
The main fortification was generally a square wooden keep or sometimes just a hall or a watchtower.

## Motte
The motte or mound could be a natural hill or else made of heaped-up soil. This steep approach to the keep made it difficult to attack.

## Stairway
The keep could be reached by a steep timber stairway. If the bailey was taken, the people could run to the keep.

## Advantages
- Wooden castles could be built quite quickly.
- Castle builders could make use of whatever materials were available locally, such as trees and soil.
- They were cheap to build and maintain.

## Disadvantages
- Wood and thatch could be easily burned down during a battle.
- Wooden castles did not have strong enough walls to resist a fierce attack.
- Wood rots, while stone walls can last for hundreds of years.

# Stone castles

From the 11th century, wooden motte-and-bailey castles were replaced with stronger defenses built of stone. The mound was now always topped with a stone keep, a high tower that was hard to attack. Over the ages, more and more stone defenses were built around the keep.

The keep at Goodrich was a square tower with thick walls built of sandstone.

**! WOW!**

Castle walls could be up to **20 feet** thick at the base.

## Building a castle

Hundreds or even thousands of laborers and craftspeople worked to build a castle. They had no modern power tools or diggers—just muscle power. Stone had to be mined and transported to the site by boat or oxcart.

**Carpenters**
Woodworkers used hammers, saws, chisels, and axes to make beams, joists, and floorboards.

**Chisel and hammer**

**Axe**

## Goodrich Castle, Hertfordshire

After the Normans conquered England in 1066, they built a wooden castle on this site. A century later, it was replaced by a stone keep, followed by outer walls and a gatehouse.

This castle was attacked in 1646 during the English Civil War. It was badly damaged, but its ruins still stand today.

## Château de Gisors

The Norman rulers of England built more than 25 castles to protect their original homeland of Normandy against the French. A wooden castle in Gisors was rebuilt with stone.

The eight-sided keep was built in 1123 by King Henry I of England.

## Scarborough Castle, Yorkshire

This castle was rebuilt in stone for Henry II of England between 1157 and 1169. It guarded the Yorkshire coast against attacks from the Scots and the French.

The stone keep was square and three stories tall.

**Masonry tools**

Treadwheel crane

Blacksmith's furnace

## Masons

Workers called masons shaped stones into walls and arches. Heavy lifting was done by wooden cranes powered by treadwheels that people turned with their feet.

**Metal tongs**

## Blacksmiths

Smiths hammered away on their anvils as they made and repaired tools, chains, and nails.

# The Great Hall

The largest room in the castle was called the Great Hall. It was the center of the household, where meetings, war conferences, or sometimes trials for criminals took place. It was a reception hall for important guests and was where banquets and entertainments were held.

**Servants**
Household servants, such as pantlers, who took care of the food pantry, attended the feast to serve the nobles.

**Salt vessel**
The nef was an ornate table decoration shaped like a ship. It was used to hold salt or spices. People on the less important tables were said to be "below the salt."

**High table**
Royalty, nobles, or other important visitors dined here, while lesser ranks ate at lower tables.

**Carved beams**
The ornate beams and roofs of the Great Hall were masterpieces of carpentry and woodwork.

**Entertainers**
Musicians might play at a feast or accompany a dance.

**Tapestry**
Wall hangings such as rich tapestries showed off the wealth and good taste of the lords and ladies.

**Give the dog a bone!**
Favorite hounds might be treated to a scrap during the meal.

# Concentric castles

Over time, castle builders added more and more defenses. These made it harder for the enemy to swarm over walls, smash through walls, or dig under them. By the 1300s, the best castles were ringed by moats and outer walls, with high inner walls and towers. We call these ring designs "concentric."

## Getting in
This castle could be accessed from the sea. It had a drawbridge, an outer gate or barbican, and a massive inner gatehouse.

## Inner bailey
The square inner bailey or ward offered access to the towers and walls, living quarters, chapel, kitchens, and water well.

## Inner wall
The second layer of defenses had huge towers and walls that were higher than the outer ones.

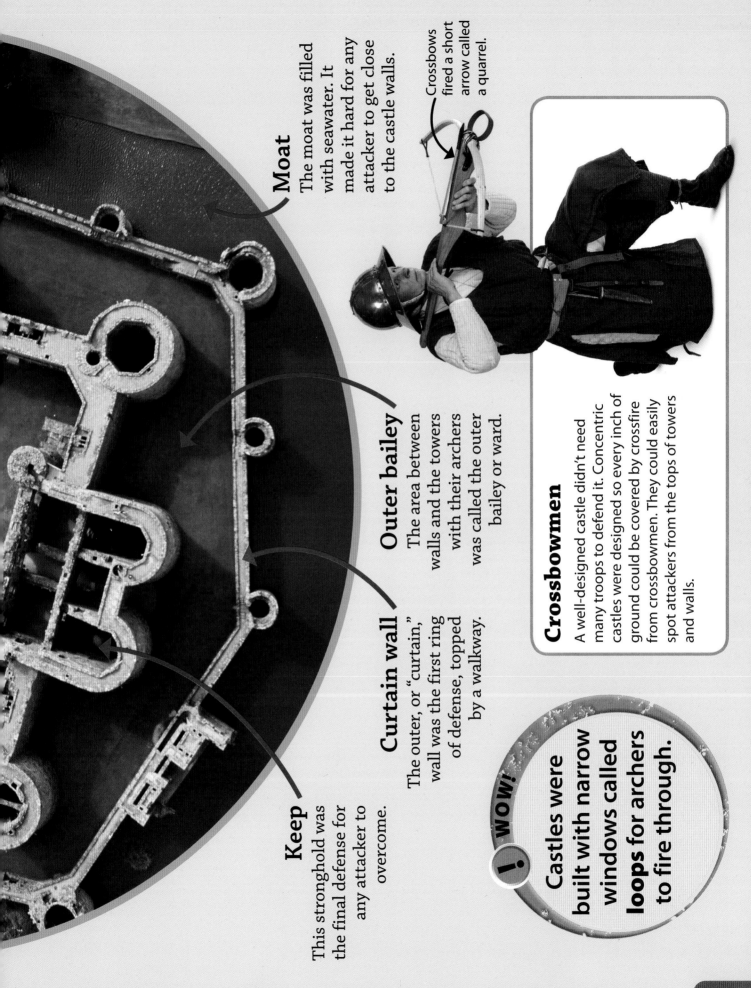

**Moat**

The moat was filled with seawater. It made it hard for any attacker to get close to the castle walls.

Crossbows fired a short arrow called a quarrel.

**Keep**

This stronghold was the final defense for any attacker to overcome.

**Curtain wall**

The outer, or "curtain," wall was the first ring of defense, topped by a walkway.

**Outer bailey**

The area between walls and the towers with their archers was called the outer bailey or ward.

## Crossbowmen

A well-designed castle didn't need many troops to defend it. Concentric castles were designed so every inch of ground could be covered by crossfire from crossbowmen. They could easily spot attackers from the tops of towers and walls.

**i** **wow!**

Castles were built with narrow windows called **loops** for archers to fire through.

# Castle defenses

The power of a castle depended on its physical strength and how fierce it looked. The building needed to be able to resist attack or capture in times of war or rebellion. Its whole structure was designed to slow down or kill any enemies who dared to attack it.

# Portcullises

This heavy grid of wood and iron was used to seal off the gatehouse. It was lowered if the castle was under attack. Sometimes, two portcullises were used together to trap the enemy in between.

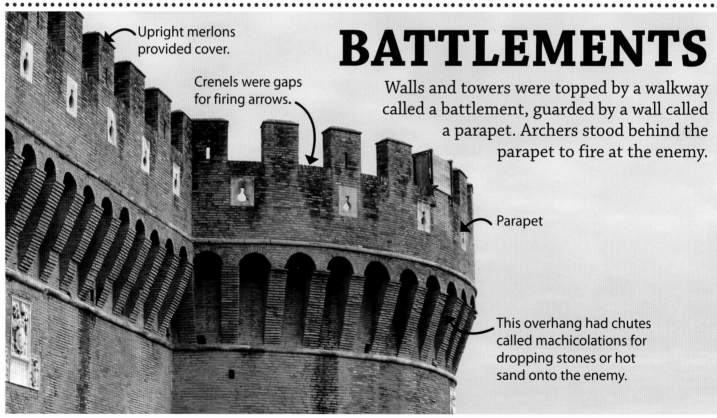

Upright merlons provided cover.

Crenels were gaps for firing arrows.

# BATTLEMENTS

Walls and towers were topped by a walkway called a battlement, guarded by a wall called a parapet. Archers stood behind the parapet to fire at the enemy.

Parapet

This overhang had chutes called machicolations for dropping stones or hot sand onto the enemy.

# MURDER HOLES

Holes in the ceiling of the gatehouse were used for dropping nasty things, such as rocks, on any enemies below. There were slits in the sides for arrows or spears.

# MOATS

Water stopped the enemy from getting too close to the walls. Moats were large ditches often filled with water and sometimes the contents of the toilets!

# Drawbridges

Drawbridges across moats and ditches could be raised to stop any unwelcome guests getting into the castle.

# TOWERS

Towers were good lookout points and were strongly built. They were awkward for invaders too—just try fighting your way up these narrow spiral stairs with a sword!

# Besieged!

The best way to capture a castle was to surround it with troops and then cut off its supplies of food and water. This was called a siege. Heavy weapons called siege engines were used to attack the castle's walls and the people inside.

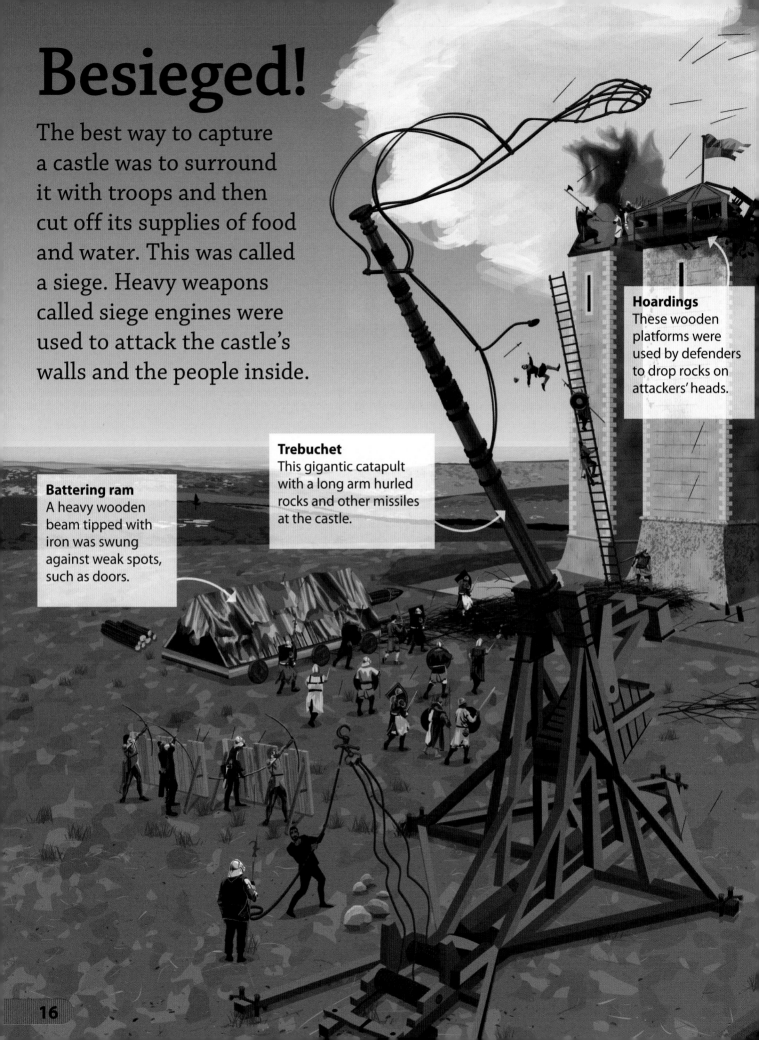

**Battering ram**
A heavy wooden beam tipped with iron was swung against weak spots, such as doors.

**Trebuchet**
This gigantic catapult with a long arm hurled rocks and other missiles at the castle.

**Hoardings**
These wooden platforms were used by defenders to drop rocks on attackers' heads.

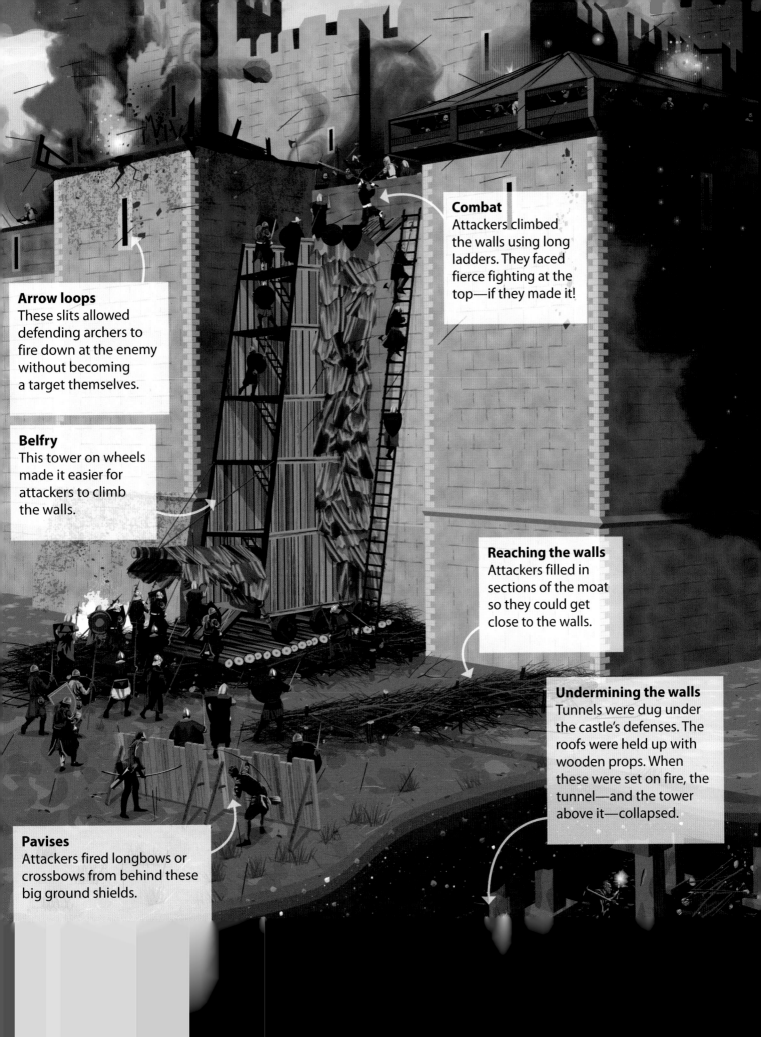

**Arrow loops**
These slits allowed defending archers to fire down at the enemy without becoming a target themselves.

**Belfry**
This tower on wheels made it easier for attackers to climb the walls.

**Pavises**
Attackers fired longbows or crossbows from behind these big ground shields.

**Combat**
Attackers climbed the walls using long ladders. They faced fierce fighting at the top—if they made it!

**Reaching the walls**
Attackers filled in sections of the moat so they could get close to the walls.

**Undermining the walls**
Tunnels were dug under the castle's defenses. The roofs were held up with wooden props. When these were set on fire, the tunnel—and the tower above it—collapsed.

# Meet the expert

Libby MacInnes is the Trebuchet Master at Warwick Castle, Warwick, UK. She tells us about what it takes to build a real-life war machine: the mighty trebuchet.

**Q: What exactly is a trebuchet?**

**A:** A trebuchet is a type of siege engine used in the medieval ages. It uses a lever (the arm) to lift a heavy counterweight in the middle. When the lever is released, gravity causes the counterweight to fall downward, lifting the lever quickly and launching its load into the air.

**Q: How big was a trebuchet?**

**A:** This would depend on the size of the trebuchet. The trebuchet at Warwick Castle is the biggest in the world at 60 feet tall and weighing 24 tons. This would have been a large trebuchet in the medieval period.

**Q: How do you know what a medieval trebuchet would have looked like or how it worked?**

**A:** Weapons were of course top secret technology and so there is very little evidence of what they looked like. However, we do have a few drawings and descriptions from history. The oldest drawing dates from 1187. We have been able to work out how trebuchets looked and worked using these sources.

**Q: How did you build the reconstructed trebuchet at Warwick Castle?**

**A:** Trebuchets were made from around 300 pieces of wood. These were made in carpentry (woodworking) workshops and transported using carts and boats, then constructed at the castle. It took around 15 people two weeks to build.

**Q: What is your favorite part of your job?**

**A:** I would have to say it is pulling the trigger for the trebuchet! We can have hundreds of people watching at our daily shows. I love to hear the sound of awe as the rock is flung at 150 miles an hour.

**Q: Do you have a favorite story from trebuchet history?**

**A:** Kind Edward I built the largest trebuchet in history, called Warwolf. He planned to use it in 1304 when he attacked the Scots at Stirling Castle. When his enemy surrendered, he missed out on using his trebuchet. He destroyed the castle gatehouse before accepting their surrender. He then charged the Scots for rebuilding the castle that now belonged to him!

Libby preparing the trebuchet to fire

Arm

**War machine**
Libby watches the
Warwick Castle
trebuchet, called
"Ursa", fire
its missile.

Counterweight

**!** **WOW!**

A trebuchet
could fire
a rock up to
**1,000 feet**.

# Dungeons

Many castles throughout history have served as prisons. With their thick walls and armed guards, any escape or rescue was difficult or impossible. People who defied the king or the Church were thrown into damp, underground dungeons full of rats and with little light or food.

**Cold and dark**
Dungeons were usually in the underground part of the castle. There might be a window with bars on it but otherwise little warming sunlight.

**The dungeon of Château de Chillon, Switzerland**
This castle dates back to 1005. In 1816, the poet Lord Byron wrote a poem called "The Prisoner of Chillon" about a monk who was imprisoned in its dungeons.

## Prison castles

Some castles became more famous as prisons than as places for lords and ladies to live. These fearsome fortresses held prisoners for the lords of other castles without a dungeon of their own.

Dürnstein Castle, Austria

Traitors' Gate

**Dürnstein Castle**
Richard I of England was held captive at Dürnstein Castle and Trifels Castle, Germany. His ransom was 100,000 pounds of silver.

**Tower of London**
The Tower of London was used as a prison up until the 20th century. Prisoners who had rebelled against the monarch were taken into the dungeons by boat through the Traitors' Gate.

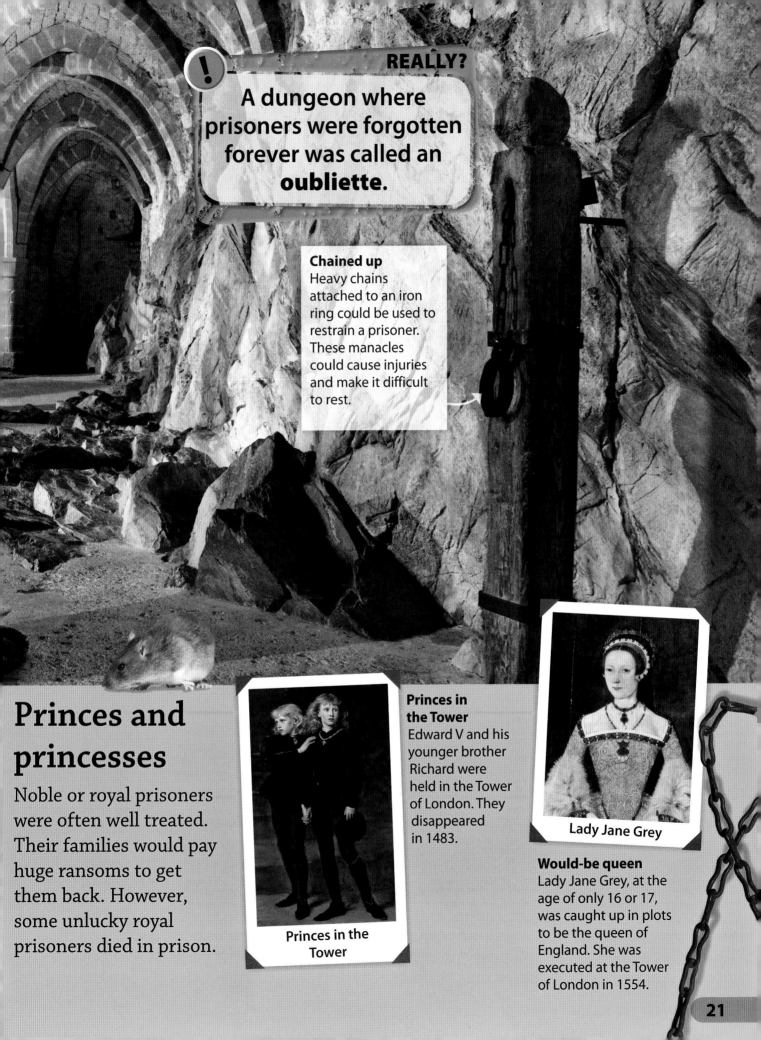

A dungeon where prisoners were forgotten forever was called an **oubliette**.

**Chained up**
Heavy chains attached to an iron ring could be used to restrain a prisoner. These manacles could cause injuries and make it difficult to rest.

# Princes and princesses

Noble or royal prisoners were often well treated. Their families would pay huge ransoms to get them back. However, some unlucky royal prisoners died in prison.

Princes in the Tower

**Princes in the Tower**
Edward V and his younger brother Richard were held in the Tower of London. They disappeared in 1483.

Lady Jane Grey

**Would-be queen**
Lady Jane Grey, at the age of only 16 or 17, was caught up in plots to be the queen of England. She was executed at the Tower of London in 1554.

# Feudal society

About 900 years ago, European society was organized in a strict order called the feudal system. Land was granted to people in return for services and loyalty to the person above you in society. The castles were power bases that helped enforce this social order.

## Monarch

A king or sometimes a queen ruled. This monarch granted castles and land to nobles in return for loyalty and military support.

**King**

## Bishop

Bishops were powerful and some had their own castles too. They sometimes quarreled with kings about powers held by the Church.

**Bishop**

## Clergy

Both nobles and poor people took up a religious life and became part of the clergy. Some lived well, while others took vows of poverty. The clergy had their own law courts.

**Friar**          **Nun**

## Law and order

As the better kings improved law and order, lawyers and court officials, such as bailiffs, were kept busy. A lot of laws were to do with buying and selling goods, made by craft workers.

**Court bailiff**

**Seamstress**

## Servants

Some poor people worked as servants and maids at the castle and in wealthier people's houses.

**Servants**

Queen

Nobles

## Vassal lords

Even powerful lords were vassals, which meant that they had to swear loyalty to the monarch.

# Serfs and villeins

Some peasants called serfs and villeins had very limited rights. They could not leave the land they worked on without permission from the lord of the castle. Being a serf was like being a slave because you did not get paid for your work.

**Serfs harvesting under the eye of a supervisor**

Knight

## Knights

Some knights became very powerful, but others were less well off. Knights fought in the service of their lord rather than for a national army.

Merchant's wife

## Craftworkers

Male merchants and craftworkers were organized into clubs called guilds, which controlled the trade. Many women also made trade goods but weren't allowed in the guilds.

Tradesman

## Peasants

Almost all poor people worked to make food. They paid their taxes by sending the lord grain or flour. Some peasants had their own land to work on, but many were serfs.

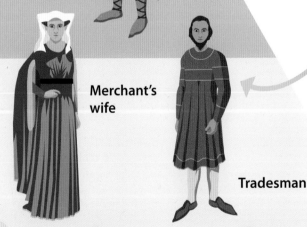

Farmers

# Lords and ladies

The lord and lady were the most powerful people in the castle, but they did not have complete power over their lands. A lord's right to own a castle was only granted to him by the king on condition of his loyalty and his military support. In turn, the lord demanded loyalty from his own followers.

## Ladies

A lady's rights were limited and she had to dress according to strict laws and fashions. She did not get to choose whom to marry. Marriages were arranged to increase a noble family's power.

## Lords

A lord's power and rank was shown by the way he dressed. There were strict laws about who had the right to wear certain materials, such as furs or silks.

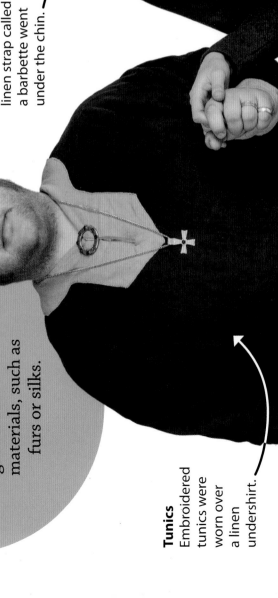

**Headdress**
Hair was tucked under a cloth called a coif. A linen strap called a barbette went under the chin.

**Tunics**
Embroidered tunics were worn over a linen undershirt.

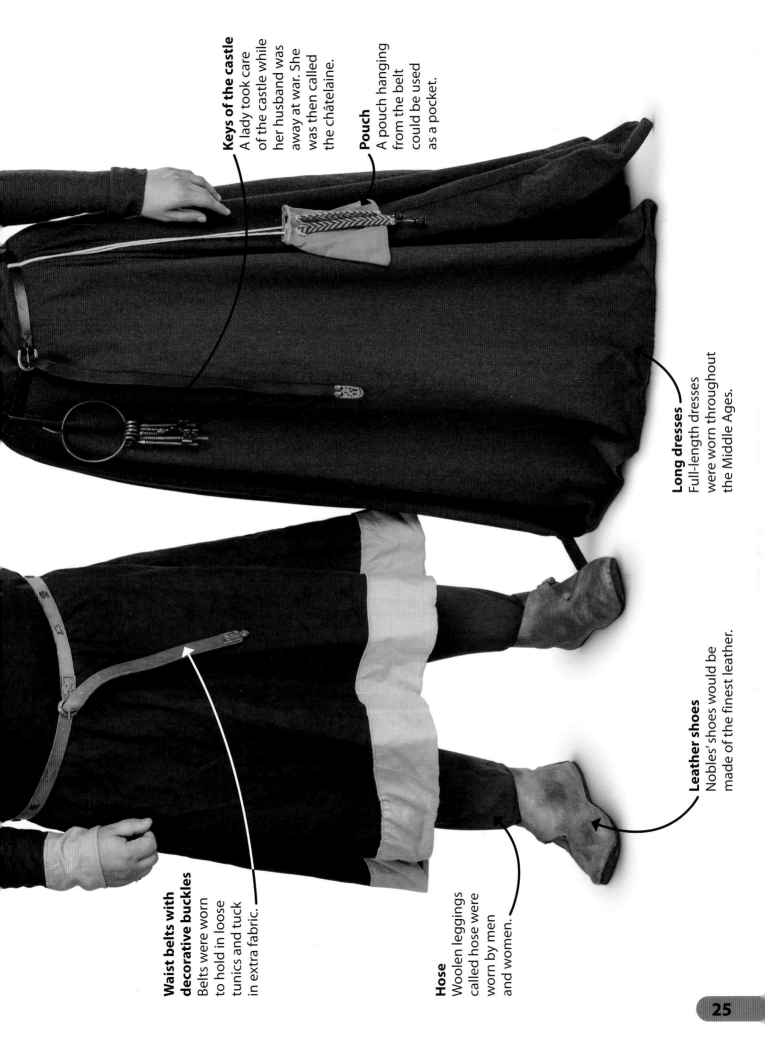

**Keys of the castle**
A lady took care of the castle while her husband was away at war. She was then called the châtelaine.

**Pouch**
A pouch hanging from the belt could be used as a pocket.

**Long dresses**
Full-length dresses were worn throughout the Middle Ages.

**Waist belts with decorative buckles**
Belts were worn to hold in loose tunics and tuck in extra fabric.

**Hose**
Woolen leggings called hose were worn by men and women.

**Leather shoes**
Nobles' shoes would be made of the finest leather.

# Working in a castle

All sorts of people worked in a castle—from people who made weapons, to cooks, maids, and cleaners. When the lord or king was there, it was busy. When an enemy army came near, many ordinary people hid within the castle walls.

**Nurse**
A nurse fed and looked after the children for the lady of the castle. Children were sometimes sent to live with other families when they were older.

**Child**
Children wore small versions of adult clothes.

**Cook**
Cooks and their assistants toiled away in the kitchens before a big banquet. Boys called scullions fetched water from the well and did the washing up.

**Cauldrons**
Stews were prepared in iron cauldrons hung from pot hooks.

**! WOW!**

The **smelliest job in the castle was cleaning out the toilet shafts and cesspits!**

**Spit**
Meat for roasting was rotated on a metal rod called a spit.

Goose feathers set at an angle

**Arrowhead**
Wooden war arrows were about 3 inches long and had long, narrow points made of iron.

**Fletcher**
A fletcher's job was to fit feathers (called fletchings) to the arrows. These made the arrow spin in flight, which made them more accurate.

**Embroidery**
Ladies often spent many hours working on beautiful embroidery. They made rich wall hangings and coverings for use in castles and churches.

**Butler**
A butler was in charge of the buttery, where butts (casks of wine or ale) were stored. He reported to the lady of the castle before a banquet.

**Stitching**
Embroiderers stitched dyed woolen thread onto linen cloth.

**Lady of the castle**
A châtelaine's duties included giving orders to the servants about what food and wine to serve.

# Peasant life

Life for poor people in medieval times was hard, especially for serfs—the poorest kind of peasant who had very few rights. Ordinary men and women had to work hard in the fields to produce food for the nobles in the castle as well as for themselves. In the 14th century, peasants across Europe rebelled against the nobles.

## Harvesting
Farming work followed the seasons. The peasants ploughed long strips of land in April, sowed the seed in May, made the hay in June, and harvested crops in August and September.

## Animals
In November, cattle, pigs, and sheep would be killed for their meat. The meat was salted to make it last throughout the winter months. Geese provided eggs and meat and were cared for by young peasant girls.

## Castle

The castle often controlled a huge area of land, including all the peasants who lived there. Nobles became rich by selling the food grown by the peasants.

## Windmill

From the 1180s, more and more windmills were built in northern Europe. Water and wind power were used to grind grain to make bread.

**Flail**
A flail was used to beat stalks of wheat until the grains separated from the inedible stems and husks.

## Chapman

Merchants or peddlers, known as chapmen, traveled from village to village selling small items such as ribbons.

## Taxes

Taxes were sums of money or food that people had to pay to the lord, the king, or the Church. The king might demand extra taxes to pay for a war.

**Medieval coins**

# Animals

Animals played an important part in everyday castle life. Horses were used for riding into battle, as transport, and when hunting. The king and nobles hunted animals, such as deer or wild boar, in the forests. Oxen hauled heavy loads and ploughed the fields.

**Beekeeping**
Beehives were kept so the castle always had honey and beeswax.

**Friesian horse**
These heavy horses are descended from medieval warhorses.

## Dogs
Dogs were bred for hunting, herding animals, and guard duties. Small pet dogs were also popular.

## Horses
The best warhorses were called destriers. Everyday riding horses were known as palfreys. Merchants used baggage horses called sumpters.

**Irish wolfhound**

## Bees

Bees provided honey, the only way to sweeten food at the time. Honey was also used in making medicines. Candles were made from beeswax.

## Falcons

Falcons and hawks were trained to hunt rabbits and other small creatures. The birds were kept in a wooden building known as the mews.

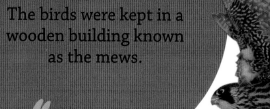
Peregrine falcon

English longhorn

## Pigeons

Pigeons were kept in huts called dovecotes and bred for eating. They were also trained to carry messages over long distances.

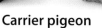
Carrier pigeon

## Stags

The male red deer, or hart, was hunted by nobles for sport. Its meat, called venison, was shared amongst them, with higher-ranked people getting more.

**Hunting party**
In some places, only the king was allowed to hunt deer.

## Cows and oxen

Cattle were raised on the castle lands, providing meat, milk for making cheese or butter, and skin for making leather.

# Dressing a knight

Knights were soldiers who rode on horseback. From the 1000s, they became valued as troops and also as high-ranking members of society. They fought in suits of armor. At first, this was mail, a mesh made from interlinking iron rings. By the 1400s, the whole body was covered in close-fitting plates of steel.

**Protective layer**
Padded shock absorbers cushioned the body against blows from axes, maces, lances, and shields.

**Coif**
This hood protected the head inside the helmet.

**Helping hands**
A servant or perhaps a squire (a trainee knight) might help the knight get kitted out before the battle or joust.

**Padding coat**
This quilted undercoat was called an aketon or gambeson. It was made of linen or wool.

**Chausses**
Mail leggings protected the legs and thighs from slashing swords.

**Sword**
The sword was designed for slashing. It had a flat, double-edged blade with a central groove.

**The great helm**
A typical European helmet looked rather like a bucket. Inside, it was padded with cloth and leather.

**Mail gloves**
These were mittens made from fine mail, with the four fingers together and a separate thumb.

**Outer layer**
This knight wears a short mail jacket, or haubergeon. A knee-length tunic with a split for mounting a horse was called a hauberk.

# Armored knight
Mail was tough and flexible, but it could be pierced. A heavy blow from a mace could cause severe bruising and injury.

# Putting on the armor
Mail fabric was made up of iron or steel rings. Each ring was linked to four others and hammered together.

**Battlefield ID**
A knight's family badge was shown on the shield and on the surcoat. It helped battlefield officials called heralds identify a knight even when his face was hidden.

**Shield**
A shield could deflect blows in battle or be used as a weapon itself.

**Surcoat**
A loose robe called a surcoat could be worn over the mail shirt.

**Scabbard**
This sheath held the blade of a sword. It hung from a belt or a shoulder strap called a baldric.

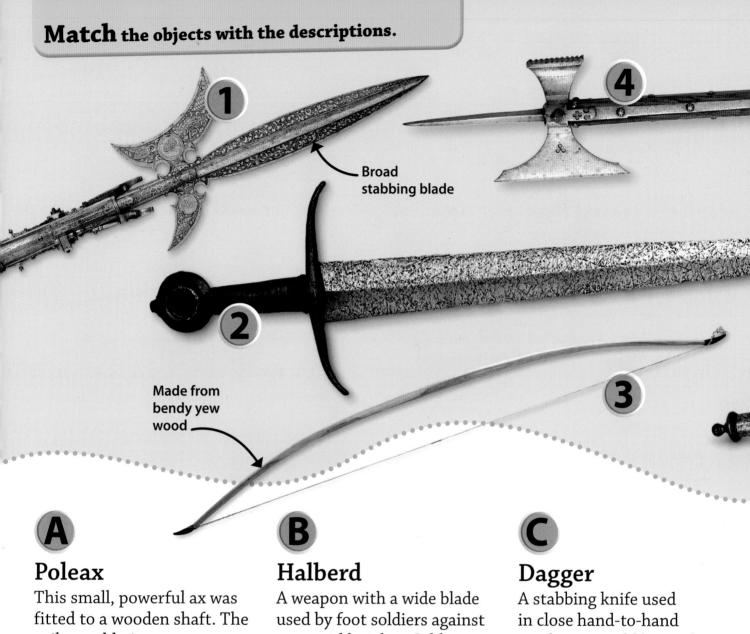

Broad stabbing blade

Made from bendy yew wood

## A

### Poleax
This small, powerful ax was fitted to a wooden shaft. The spike could pierce armor and the blade could be used for slashing.

## B

### Halberd
A weapon with a wide blade used by foot soldiers against mounted knights. Soldiers used the hooked part to drag knights off their horses.

## C

### Dagger
A stabbing knife used in close hand-to-hand combat. It could be easily hidden for a secret attack.

# Name your weapon!

A medieval battle was brutal. Longbows could injure an enemy soldier up to about 650 feet away. Mounted fighters, called the cavalry, used lances, slashing swords, battle axes, and maces. Foot soldiers used pole weapons to try to dismount the knights, whose heavy armor made them slow on the ground.

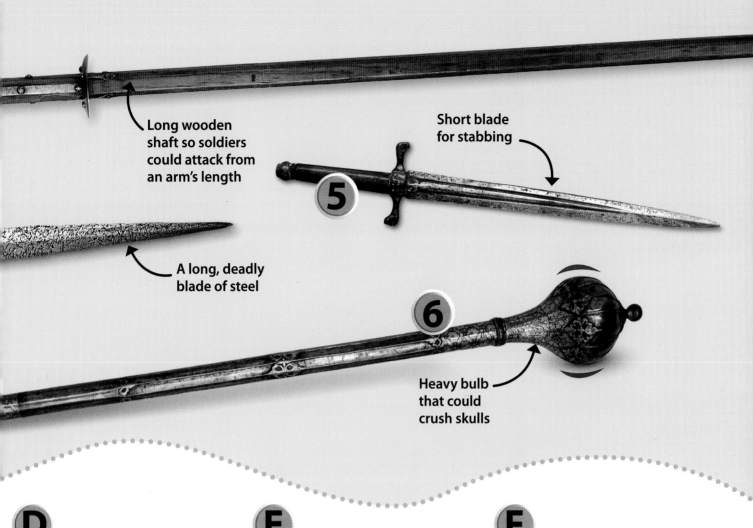

**Long wooden shaft so soldiers could attack from an arm's length**

**Short blade for stabbing**

**5**

**A long, deadly blade of steel**

**6**

**Heavy bulb that could crush skulls**

## D

# Mace

The mace was a kind of club with a heavy, round head. It was used by both foot soldiers and knights.

## E

# Longbow

Medieval archers used the longbow to fire deadly showers of arrows into the enemy lines before the two sides closed in battle. Welsh archers were famous for their skills.

## F

# Sword

Swords could be used in close combat by foot soldiers and also by knights on horseback. Some were designed for thrusting and stabbing; others for slashing.

**! WOW!**

**At the Battle of Agincourt in 1415, English archers fired 1,000 arrows per second.**

## Battle of the bows

Genoese archers were the masters of the crossbow. They fought for the French against the English at the Battle of Crécy. However, crossbows were much slower to reload than longbows and the English triumphed.

**Battle of Crécy, 1346**

# Tournaments

The medieval tournament was a display of riding and fighting skills. Knights competed to be the winners. The first tournaments were held around the time stone castles began to be built in the 11th century. By the 1500s, they had become grand and colorful spectacles.

## Jousting

The joust recreated a real battle. Two mounted knights thundered toward each other in full armor. Their long, blunt lance might break on the opponent's shield or a knight might be knocked off his horse. It was dangerous.

## Clashes of arms

Popular forms of combat included fights between teams of mounted knights or mass brawls on foot. Some were violent free-for-alls in which every man fought for himself.

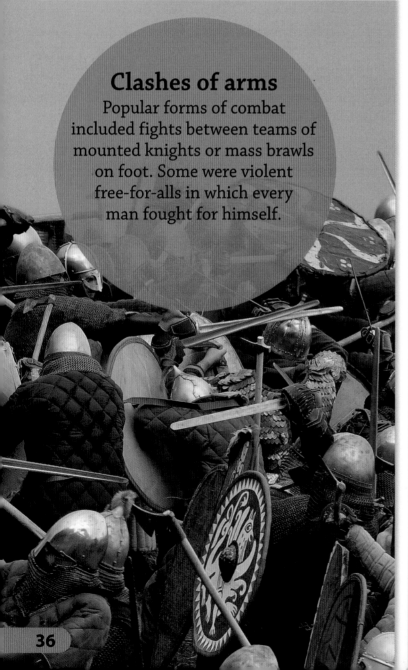

# Heraldic symbols

By the end of the Middle Ages, tournaments were places to show off fancy armor, plumed helmets, and flags. Heraldic symbols were a noble family's favorite images of power, such as dragons and castles. They appeared on surcoats, shields, and on the horses' coverings.

**Heraldic designs**

## Lady's favor

A lady might agree for a particular knight to fight as a champion of her honor, wearing her scarf or ribbon in the joust. This was part of the knight's code of honor, known as chivalry.

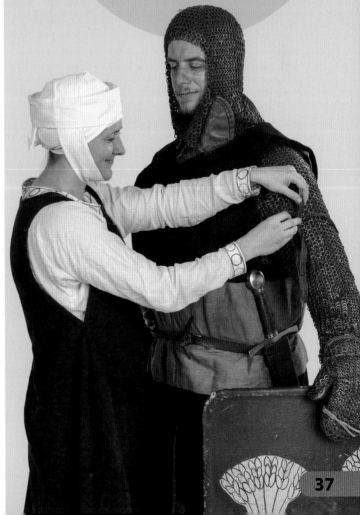

37

# Food and feasts

In the Middle Ages, food was grown close to where people lived. Country people would often pay their taxes "in kind," which meant sending in food to the castle. If bad weather or a marauding army destroyed the crops, many people went hungry.

## Cutlery

People took their own knives or spoons to a meal. Forks became popular in Italy in the 1300s and then spread to the rest of Europe.

## Food for the peasants

Everyday meals might be just a crust of gritty bread with cheese or a bowl of thin porridge. Peasants also caught fish and rabbits and raised geese to roast for special feasts.

**Cheese**

**Pottage**

**Stew**
Pottages were thick stews of vegetables or meat.

**Trenchers**
Food was often served on a trencher, a round, flat piece of bread.

In the days before refrigeration, foods were preserved by salting, smoking, pickling, or drying.

**Pickled herring**

**Bacon**

38

# Food for the lords

A special banquet would be held in the Great Hall for a visiting lord or bishop. It might include wild boar, venison (deer meat), swan, wild birds, fish, and fine white bread.

**Spices**
Spices were beginning to be imported from Asia at great expense.

Saffron

Peppercorns

Nutmeg

Cinnamon

Ginger

Boar's head with apples

**Elaborate decorations**
Food was served in all sorts of decorative ways to make it look as expensive as possible.

Roasted almonds

Apple pie

Pheasant meat

Berry and rose petal rice pudding

# Entertainment

Medieval festivals, such as May Day, were celebrated with music and dancing. Entertainers, such as acrobats and jugglers, traveled from one castle to another to perform. The surrounding towns put on "mystery plays" in which local people acted out stories from the Bible.

## INSTRUMENTS

Medieval people had no recorded music! It was performed live on harps, lutes, flutes, trumpets, drums, or bagpipes. Many of these developed over the ages into the instruments we know today.

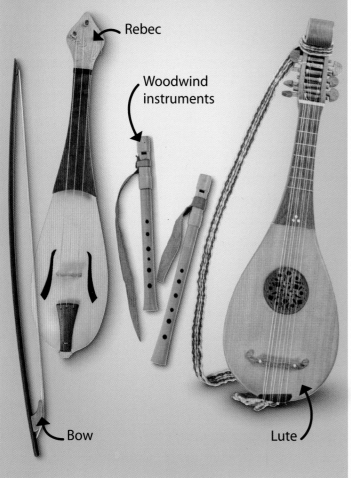

Rebec

Woodwind instruments

Bow

Lute

The lute came to Europe from the Middle East.

A musical pipe called the recorder became popular in the 1200s.

## Minstrels and troubadours

Minstrels (musicians) might perform in the Great Hall of the castle during a feast. From the 1100s to the 1350s, poets called troubadours toured the castles of southern France, singing of chivalry and courtly love.

## Court jester

The jester was a bit like a modern stand-up comedian. He was kept by the nobles to make fun of powerful people, tell jokes, and talk entertaining nonsense.

# MUMMERS

During winter festivals, such as Christmas, masked performers called mummers would roam the streets or go from house to house, making music.

## DANCING

Country people liked jolly dances with a lot of spinning around, clapping, and stamping. Villagers might dance in a ring, holding hands. At the castle, the nobles preferred stately dances, pacing, pointing toes, skipping, and curtseying.

## Indoor games

Chess was invented in India, but the European board game developed between about 1100 to 1475. Its pieces reflect medieval life, with castles, knights, kings and queens, and bishops.

Chess pieces

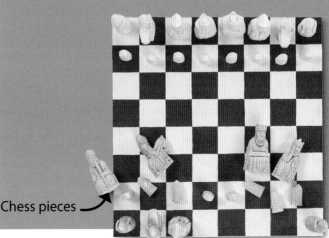

# Prayer and worship

During the Middle Ages, most of Europe, apart from Muslim Spain, was known as Christendom. Every part of daily life was affected by religious beliefs. The center of religious life in a castle was the chapel, where people went to pray and hear readings from the Bible.

Hugues de Payens founded the order of the Knights Templar in 1119.

## Abbeys and monasteries

Just as castles controlled people's working lives, religious faith was organized around buildings, such as abbeys and monasteries. International orders of monks were often more powerful and wealthy than kings. The island abbey of Mont-St-Michel in Normandy was even fortified like a castle.

Mont-St-Michel, Normandy, France

## Warrior monks

Between 1096 and 1291, popes called for "Crusades"—holy wars usually fought against Muslims. Knights gathered together into religious groups, such as the Knights Templar, and went to fight abroad.

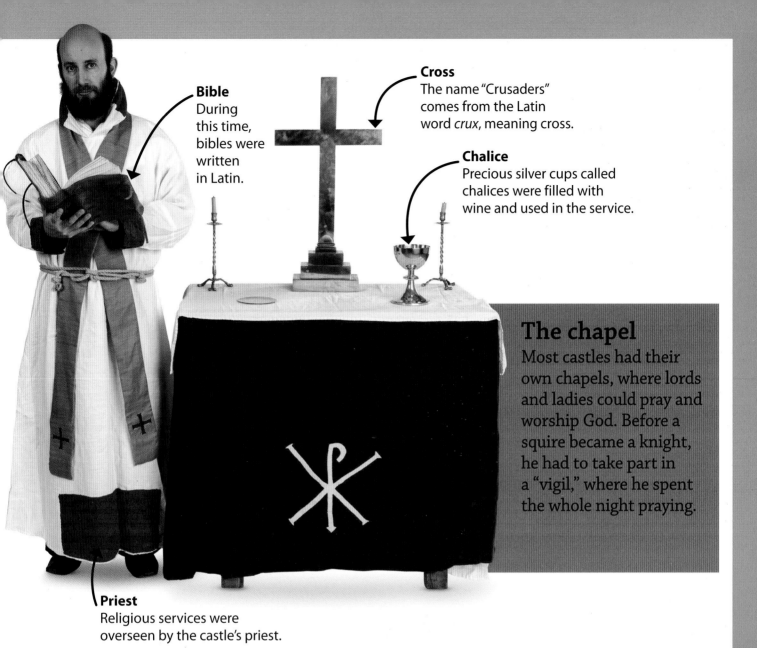

**Bible**
During this time, bibles were written in Latin.

**Cross**
The name "Crusaders" comes from the Latin word *crux*, meaning cross.

**Chalice**
Precious silver cups called chalices were filled with wine and used in the service.

## The chapel
Most castles had their own chapels, where lords and ladies could pray and worship God. Before a squire became a knight, he had to take part in a "vigil," where he spent the whole night praying.

**Priest**
Religious services were overseen by the castle's priest.

# Religious wars

As well as wars against other religions, there were many bitter conflicts between Christians. From 1209 to 1229, the pope held a crusade against the Cathars, a Christian group in southern France. Knights carried out massacres against the Cathar people.

Carcassonne, a Cathar stronghold

Cathars are forced out of Carcassonne in 1209.

# Castles in Europe

The Middle Ages were a time of brutal warfare, which meant that thousands of castles were built across the kingdoms of Europe. Castles were crucial during battles to be king, wars over land and religion, and peasants' revolts.

## Marksburg Castle

This famous castle towers high above the Rhine river. It has seen many conflicts, up to World War II. It has been rebuilt several times—but never destroyed.

FACT FILE

» **Built in:** 1117

» **Location:** Braubach, Rhineland-Palatinate, Germany

## Château Gaillard

This castle was built by King Richard I, "the Lionheart". During a siege in 1203–04, a French soldier managed to enter the castle by climbing in through a toilet chute!

FACT FILE

» **Built in:** 1196–98

» **Location:** Les Andelys, Normandy, France

# Fénis Castle

With fancy battlements, Fénis looks more luxurious than many castles. In the 1390s, it had its own vineyard to provide wine.

**FACT FILE**

» **Built in:** 1242–1420

» **Location:** Aosta Valley, Italy

# Będzin Castle

Before Będzin, there was a wooden castle that was destroyed when the Tatars invaded in 1241. The stone castle was built by King Casimir the Great of Poland.

**FACT FILE**

» **Built in:** 1348

» **Location:** Silesian Highlands, Poland

**FACT FILE**

» **Built in:** 1475

» **Location:** Community of Madrid, Spain

# Manzanares el Real New Castle

This fine castle replaced an older fortress (the "Old Castle"). It was built when the Middle Ages were coming to an end, so it came to be used more as a luxurious palace than for defense.

# Moorish castles

From the year 711, Muslim armies from northwest Africa invaded Spain and Portugal. A group called the Moors founded a country called al-Andalus and fought their way into France. They built many castles. By 1492, these lands had been reconquered by Christian armies.

**Salon de Embajadores**
This square tower is 150 feet high. It contains a splendid throne room built from 1334 to 1354.

**Alhambra, Spain**
From 889 to the 1400s, this fort became a castle and a palace. It towers over Granada, Spain.

## Beautiful defences

Many Moorish castles have strong square towers linked to city walls. Later, they developed into palaces with beautifully decorated courtyards, fountains, and gardens.

**Arches**
The Moors were skilled architects and craft workers. Arches were built in curves and keyhole shapes.

**Domes**
Domes and arched ceilings with intricate designs created wonderful spaces inside council chambers, throne rooms, and mosques.

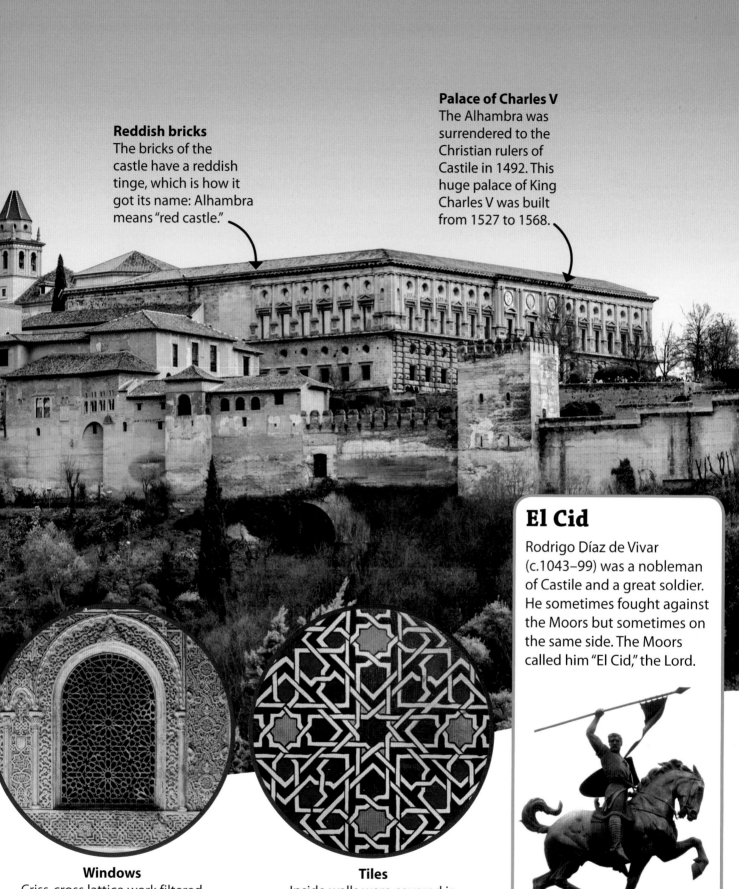

**Reddish bricks**
The bricks of the castle have a reddish tinge, which is how it got its name: Alhambra means "red castle."

**Palace of Charles V**
The Alhambra was surrendered to the Christian rulers of Castile in 1492. This huge palace of King Charles V was built from 1527 to 1568.

**Windows**
Criss-cross lattice work filtered out the blazing Spanish sun or allowed in a gentle breeze. Splashing fountains cooled the hot air.

**Tiles**
Inside walls were covered in colorful tiles with complicated geometrical patterns to dazzle the eye. Some walls displayed calligraphy (beautiful writing).

# El Cid

Rodrigo Díaz de Vivar (c.1043–99) was a nobleman of Castile and a great soldier. He sometimes fought against the Moors but sometimes on the same side. The Moors called him "El Cid," the Lord.

**Statue of El Cid**

# Crusader castles

Many castles still stand in southwest Asia and the Middle East from the time of the Crusades (1096–1291). These wars were fought between west European Christians and Muslim armies. They were about religion and control of trade and land. Both sides used castles, which were often captured and recaptured.

**Krak des Chevaliers**
This castle in Syria was built by the Emir of Homs in 1031. It was captured by Crusaders in 1099.

**Big slope**
These steep walls or "taluses" shored up the towers against earthquakes and made it hard to undermine or climb.

## Lands and knights

The Holy Land in the Middle East was sacred to Jews, Christians, and Muslims. New kingdoms created by invading Crusaders were referred to as Outremer ("overseas"). Crusaders called the Muslims "Saracens", while the Muslims called the Europeans "Franks."

**Knight Templar**

**Crusading orders**
Religious orders of knights included the Knights Hospitaller, who held the Krak des Chevaliers, and the Knights Templar, who had their base at the Temple Mount, a holy place in Jerusalem.

**Inner ward**
Within the inner ward were living quarters, stores, a great hall, and a chapel.

**!** **REALLY?**

**Krak des Chevaliers could house a huge garrison of about 2,000 men.**

**Strong outer walls**
This outer wall was added in the 13th century, making it a concentric castle.

**Water supply**
Droughts were common in Syria. An aqueduct channeled water into an inner moat, which also served as a reservoir for drinking water.

Saladin

**Salah ad-Din**
This Kurdish sultan of Egypt reigned from 1174 to 1193. He was a military commander who won the respect of many Europeans with his brilliance. They called him "Saladin."

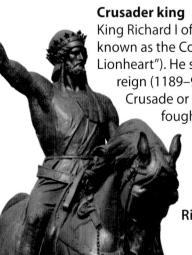

**Crusader king**
King Richard I of England was known as the Coeur de Lion ("the Lionheart"). He spent most of his reign (1189–99) on the Third Crusade or in captivity. He fought against Saladin in the Third Crusade.

Richard the Lionheart

49

# End of an age

By the 1300s, the feudal system was breaking down in western Europe. Under the feudal system, power had been based on land rather than on money. As trade became more important, a banker could become richer than a king. During wars, the mighty stone walls of castles couldn't withstand powerful new weapons.

Ruins of Corfe Castle, England

## End of feudalism

In 1215, English barons forced King John to give away many of his royal powers by putting his seal on a document called the Magna Carta. This began to break down the feudal system that was so important in running castles.

King John and the Magna Carta

## What happened to the castles?

Some castles were "slighted," which means badly damaged by the enemy so they could not be used. Some were abandoned. Few castles were used after the 1650s and they fell into ruin.

## The plague

In 1347, a plague arrived in Europe. The "Black Death" killed about 50 million people, so there weren't enough left to work on the land. Peasants could now demand high wages instead of working for the lord for free.

People bringing out their plague dead for burial

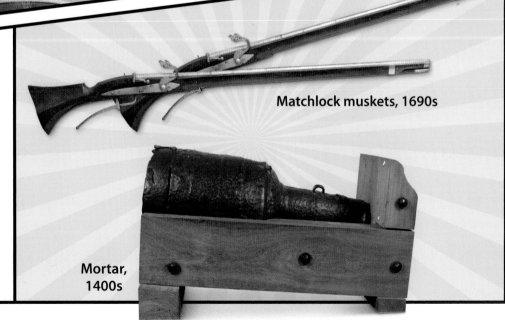

Louvre Palace, France

## Rise of palaces

In 1360, King Charles V of France converted the Louvre Castle, which defended Paris, into a grand palace. Many kings now deserted their damp, draughty castles and moved into luxurious city palaces.

## Gunpowder

Simple cannons were being used in Europe in the 1300s. By the 1460s, they were powerful enough to destroy stone walls. Castles became useless, as the people inside were no longer safe from siege.

Matchlock muskets, 1690s

Mortar, 1400s

# Japanese castles

Castles first developed in Japan during the Middle Ages. From the 1400s to the 1600s, powerful lords called the daimyo replaced simple forts made of timber and mud with grand, towering castles. These played an important part in Japan's history as rival clans battled for power.

**White Heron Castle**
This name was given to Himeji Castle because of its elegant white towers.

**Himeji castle**
Japan's largest castle, Himeji, was built in 1581 by Toyotomi Hideyoshi. He was a famous warrior, daimyo, and castle builder.

# Samurai warriors

The Samurai, or Bushi, were warriors who served a lord. From the 1100s to the 1800s, they were elite troops with a high social status. They followed a strict code of honor, known as Bushido.

**Sumptuous quarters**
The upper level of the castle contained the lord's living quarters. They would have been luxurious.

Horned helmet

War mask

**Armor**
Samurai armor, called yoroi, was made up of iron scales and plates coated in shiny lacquer and tied together with cords of silk.

Armored skirt

Wakizashi

Katana

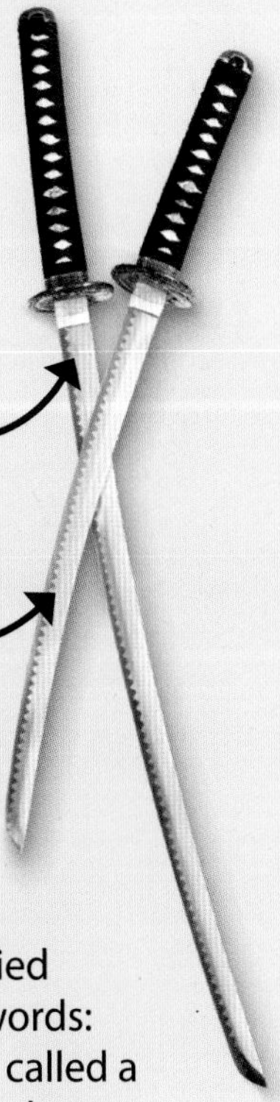

**Swords**
Samurai carried two sharp swords: a longer one called a katana and a shorter one called a wakizashi.

**Shin guards**

# Fantasy castles

In the 1400s, kings, queens, and nobles liked to imagine they were living in magical castles with turrets and spires. Their minstrels and poets told stories about legendary castles. In the 1800s, some people actually built romantic fairytale castles.

Present-day Château de Saumur, by the Loire river, France

## Neuschwanstein Castle

King Ludwig II of Bavaria, Germany, was a dreamer who loved music and architecture. His ultimate romantic fantasy was this hilltop castle, which was built from 1869 to 1886.

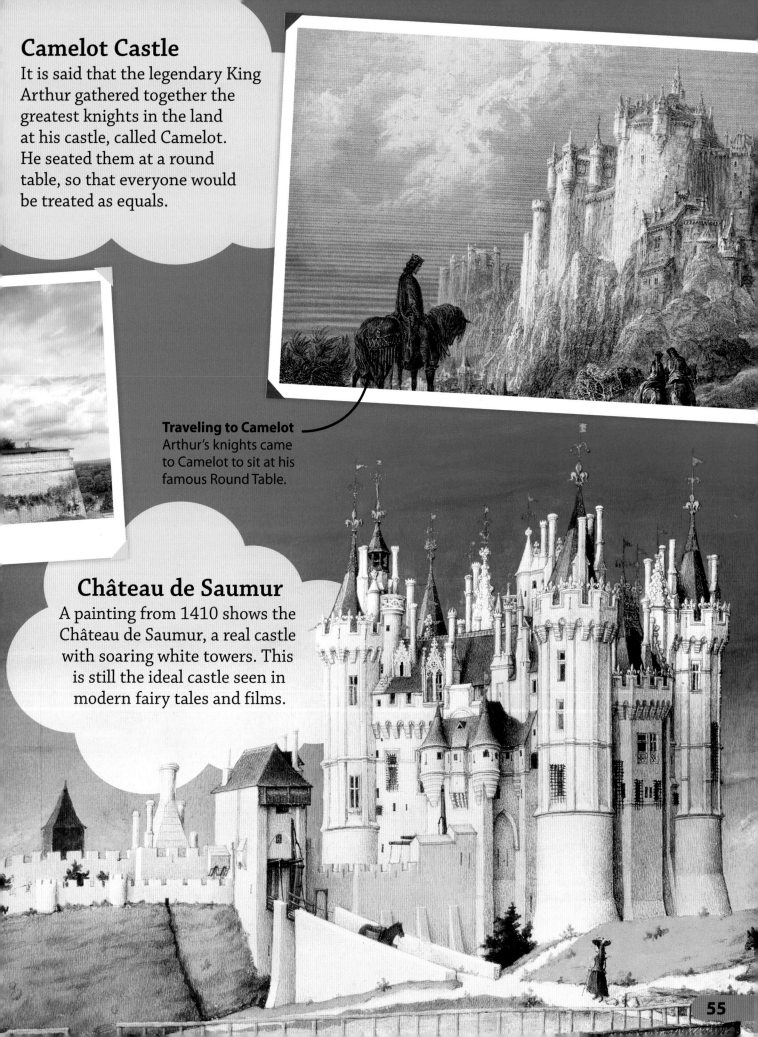

## Camelot Castle

It is said that the legendary King Arthur gathered together the greatest knights in the land at his castle, called Camelot. He seated them at a round table, so that everyone would be treated as equals.

**Traveling to Camelot**
Arthur's knights came to Camelot to sit at his famous Round Table.

## Château de Saumur

A painting from 1410 shows the Château de Saumur, a real castle with soaring white towers. This is still the ideal castle seen in modern fairy tales and films.

# Myths and legends

Every castle has its own amazing real-life story, but people love to tell fanciful tales about them too. Some of these are about knights and heroines; some about magical beasts and supernatural beings. Over time, the true stories have become legends.

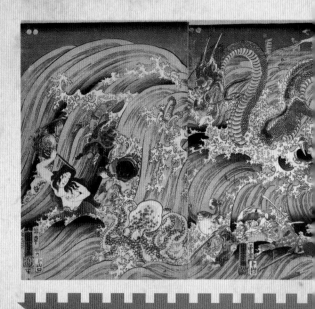

## Robin Hood

This legendary outlaw from England "robbed the rich to pay the poor." His greatest enemy was the evil sheriff who lived in Nottingham Castle.

Vlad III

## Legend of Dracula

A cruel medieval prince called Vlad III lived in the castles of Bran, Poenari, and Hunyadi in 15th-century Romania. In the 1800s, a writer called Bram Stoker based his vampire Dracula on Vlad.

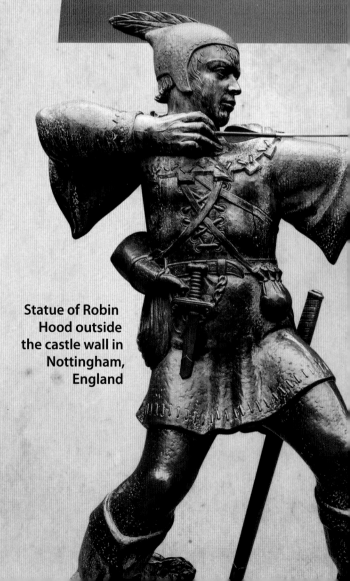

Statue of Robin Hood outside the castle wall in Nottingham, England

## Dragon king

In Japanese folk tales, a castle belonging to a dragon called Ryujin lies under the sea. One day spent in this palace is the same as 100 years in the outside world.

The dragon Ryujin

The princess is rescued by her brother.

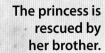

**Robin Hood has featured in at least 78 films and TV series.**

## Laidley Wyrm

A king was living at Bamburgh Castle when his wife died. He got married again, to a witch. She turned her new stepdaughter, the princess, into a dragon called the "Laidley Wyrm."

The ruins of Tintagel, Cornwall, England

## King Arthur

If Arthur ever existed, he was probably a war leader who died in about 537 CE. In the later Middle Ages, storytellers reinvented him as a great king. They said that the wizard Merlin was there when Arthur was born at Tintagel Castle.

# Facts and figures

Castles impressed and intimidated the world for hundreds of years. Even though many of them are now in ruins, we still find them amazing. Read on to learn facts and figures about castles.

**PLATE ARMOR SUITS** were given as top prizes in tournaments. German armor was considered the finest and stamped with the armorer's trademark.

Most people in the Middle Ages went without breakfast. The main meal of the day was around mid-morning, at about **10 or 11 o'clock**.

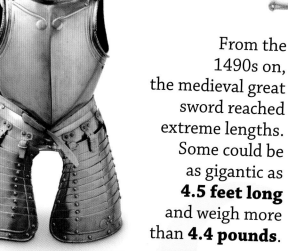

From the 1490s on, the medieval great sword reached extreme lengths. Some could be as gigantic as **4.5 feet long** and weigh more than **4.4 pounds**.

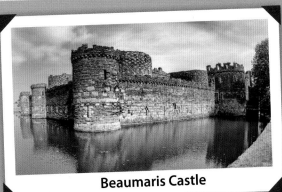
Beaumaris Castle

**BEAUMARIS CASTLE** in Wales cost about $20,000 to build more than seven centuries ago. In today's money, that would be about $20.3 million.

# 10,000

castles are recorded to have been built in Spain over the ages. About 2,500 of them still survive.

Rumelian Castle dungeon,
Istanbul, Turkey

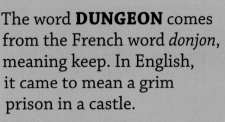

The word **DUNGEON** comes from the French word *donjon*, meaning keep. In English, it came to mean a grim prison in a castle.

The medieval longbow was up to about **6 feet** long and had a range of more than **1,025 feet.**

### The path to knighthood

began with young boys who served as **pages** in the castle, then as **squires** who assisted knights. When they learned how to fight they finally became **knights**.

# 300-POUND

boulders could be thrown by the Warwolf, the biggest trebuchet ever built. It was made for King Edward I of England and used during the siege of Stirling Castle, Scotland.

# 12 YEARS

was how long it took the Ottoman Turks to win the Siege of Philadelphia in modern-day Turkey. It lasted from 1378 to 1390.

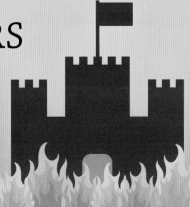

# Glossary

Here are the meanings of some words that are useful for you to know when learning all about medieval castles.

**armory** Place where armor and weapons were kept

**bailey** Also known as a ward, this was an open space inside a castle's walls

**battlement** Walkway at the top of a castle wall designed to help with defense

**Bushido** Code of honor used by samurai warriors

**butler** Servant who took care of wine and ale

**carpenter** Craftworker who made things out of wood

**chapman** Merchant or salesman who went between villages selling small items

**châtelaine** Woman who took care of a castle where there was no lord

**crossbow** Medieval bow that fired short bolts

**chivalry** Code of honor used by medieval European knights

**coif** Close-fitting cap made of cloth or mail

**concentric** A type of castle with inner and outer walls

**crusade** Religious war agreed to by a Christian pope

**Daimyo** Japanese feudal lords

**destrier** Warhorse of a medieval knight

**drawbridge** Bridge that could be pulled up to stop attackers from entering

**dungeon** Castle prison, usually dark, damp, and cold

**feudalism** System where people owed loyalty to those with more wealth and power

**fletcher** Craftworker who made arrows

**garrison** Group of soldiers living in a castle

**halberd** Type of long weapon used for stabbing and cutting

**heraldry** Symbols and colors worn by a knight

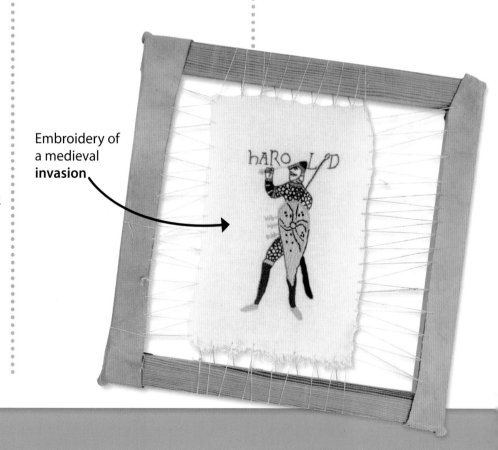

Embroidery of a medieval **invasion**

**invasion** Large-scale attack by a foreign army

**jester** Court servant who told jokes and silly stories

**jousting** Sport where knights tried to knock each other off horses using long poles called lances

**keep** Most secure and fortified part of a castle

**knight** Warrior who fought on horseback

**longbow** Medieval bow that could fire arrows a long way

**lute** Stringed musical instrument

**mace** Hand weapon with a heavy or spiked head

**mail** Links of metal connected together to make armor

**motte** Mound of earth that made a good place to build a keep

**moat** Ditch around a castle, either dry or filled with water

**mummer** Performer who traveled around villages playing music for money

**murder hole** Hole in a castle gatehouse that let defenders drop rocks on attackers

**nef** Salt cellar shaped like a ship

**oubliette** Tiny prison cell where prisoners might be forgotten about

**palfrey** Ordinary horses used for riding

**palisade** Wooden wall built to protect a motte-and-bailey castle

**pantler** Servant who took care of food stores and the pantry

**parapet** Wall along the top of a battlement

**pavise** Large shield that defended archers on the battlefield

**poleax** Weapon with a long pole and a stabbing and cutting blade on the end

**portcullis** Gate that could be lowered to cut off a castle entrance

**pottage** Thick vegetable or meat stew eaten by peasants

Heraldic shield

**Samurai** Japanese warriors

**scabbard** Sheath to carry a sword in

**serf** Medieval peasant who was not paid for their work

**sumpter** Horse that was used by merchants to carry goods

**surcoat** Tunic worn by a knight over his armor

**tapestry** Woven decorative cloth

**trebuchet** Giant catapult that could fire rocks hundreds of feet

**trencher** Bread used as a plate in medieval times

# Index

# Acknowledgments

The publishers would like to thank: Helen Peters for the index; Richard Leeney for photography; Dan Crisp for illustrations; Jolyon Goddard, Sally Beets, Abi Luscombe and Lori Hand for editorial help; and The Household for modelling: Ben Phillips, Andy Everett, Edward Tyson, Sophie Tyson, Tom Chadwick, Boyd Chester-Freeman, Martin Howell, Graham Wellard, Karl Perry, Jay Holland, Mark Graves, Rebecca Tyson, Peter Farmer, Isobel Sheldon, and especially Rebecca Tyson. Additional thanks to Tom Chadwick for historical consultation.

The publisher would like to thank the following for their kind permission to reproduce their photographs:

(Key: a-above; b-below/bottom; c-center; f-far; l-left; r-right; t-top)

**2 Alamy Stock Photo:** North Wind Picture Archives (cb). **Dorling Kindersley:** The Combined Military Services Museum (CMSM) (bl). **3 Alamy Stock Photo:** Paul Street (clb). Dreamstime.com: Sederi (tr). **4-5 Alamy Stock Photo:** Valery Egorov. **8-9 Alamy Stock Photo:** Adrian Campbell-Burt (t). **8 Alamy Stock Photo:** Gennadiy Guchek (bc). Dreamstime.com: Draghicich (br). **9 Alamy Stock Photo:** Arterra Picture Library (clb); Paul Street (tr); Panther Media GmbH (crb). **Dorling Kindersley:** National Guild of Stone Masons and Carvers, London (fbl); University Museum of Archaeology and Anthropology, Cambridge (bc). **Dreamstime.com:** Svlumagraphica (bl). Getty Images: Loop Images / UIG (cr). **10** 123RF.com: flik47 (crb). **10-11 Dorling Kindersley:** Weald and Downland Open Air Museum, Chich (b). **Getty Images:** VisitBritain / Daniel Bosworth. **The Metropolitan Museum of Art:** Gift of John D. Rockefeller Jr., 1937 (cb). **12-13 Alamy Stock Photo:** robertharding. **14 Dreamstime.com:** Alessandro0770 (bl). **iStockphoto.com:** rsaraiva (tr). **15 Alamy Stock Photo:** A.P.S. (UK) (cra); Manor Photography (cla); Steve Taylor ARPS (cr). **Dreamstime.com:** Arenaphotouk (bl). **18 Libby MacInnes:** (tl). **19 Andy Sallis Photography:** (tr). **20 Alamy Stock Photo:** volkerpreusser (cb). **Dreamstime.com:** Felix Bensman (crb). **20-21 Alamy Stock Photo:** FB-StockPhoto-1. **21 Alamy Stock Photo:** GL Archive (bc); Granger Historical Picture Archive (crb). 23 Alamy Stock Photo: Granger Historical Picture Archive (cra). **26 Dorling Kindersley:** The Science Museum, London (bc). **29 Dreamstime.com:** Salih Külcü (tr). **30 Rex by Shutterstock:**

Gianni Dagli Orti (tr). **31 Alamy Stock Photo:** F1online digitale Bildagentur GmbH (cla). **Dorling Kindersley:** Cotswold Farm Park, Gloucestershire (cr). **Dreamstime.com:** Sederi (tr). Rex by Shutterstock: Universal History Archive / UIG (bc). **32-33 Dreamstime.com:** Sfocato (b). 34 Dorling Kindersley: © The Board of Trustees of the Armouries (tl, c). **34-35 Dorling Kindersley:** Wallace Collection, London (ca, t). **35 Alamy Stock Photo:** Archivah (br). **Dorling Kindersley:** The Combined Military Services Museum (CMSM) (cra). **The Metropolitan Museum of Art:** Gift of Christian A. Zabriskie, 1936 (ca). **36 Getty Images:** NurPhoto (bl). 36-37 **Dreamstime.com:** Tracy King (c). **37 Alamy Stock Photo:** North Wind Picture Archives (tr). **38 123RF.com:** dipalipix (tr). **Dreamstime.com:** Kiboka (bl); Subodh Sathe (ca). **iStockphoto.com:** cobraphoto (crb). **39 Dreamstime.com:** Anlooka (c); Eyeblink (ca); Gary Smith (clb). **41 Alamy Stock Photo:** M&N (cr). Getty Images: Christophel Fine Art / UIG (tl). **42 Alamy Stock Photo:** Heritage Image Partnership Ltd (tr). **Dreamstime.com:** Ivan Soto (b). **43 Alamy Stock Photo:** imageBROKER (cb); Niday Picture Library (crb). **44 Alamy Stock Photo:** Hemis (bl). **Dreamstime.com:** Ruth Peterkin (cr). 45 **Dreamstime.com:** Marco Saracco (cra). **iStockphoto.com:** ewg3D (cr); TomasSereda (bl). **46-47 Dreamstime.com:** Stelios Kyriakides. **46 Dreamstime.com:** Neirfy (cb). **47 Dorling Kindersley:** Casino Espanol (cb). iStockphoto.com: caracterdesign (clb). **48 Alamy Stock Photo:** Holmes Garden Photos (bc). **48-49 Alamy Stock Photo:** robertharding (t). **49 Alamy Stock Photo:** PjrStatues (br). SuperStock: World History Archive (bl). **50 Alamy Stock Photo:** Commission Air (cl); Pictorial Press Ltd (br). **51 Alamy Stock Photo:** Granger Historical Picture Archive (tr). **Dorling Kindersley:** Royal Artillery, Woolwich (br); The Combined Military Services Museum (CMSM) (crb).

Dreamstime.com: Rostislav Ageev (cl). **52-53 Alamy Stock Photo:** Ian Macpherson Japan. **53 Alamy Stock Photo:** maxstock (br). **Dorling Kindersley:** Maidstone Museum and Bentliff Art Gallery (c, bc). **54 Dreamstime.com:** Minnystock. **54-55 Dreamstime.com:** Ivan Soto (c). **55 Getty Images:** Christophel Fine Art / UIG. **iStockphoto.com:** duncan1890 (tr). **56 Getty Images:** Stefano Bianchetti / Corbis (clb). **56-57 Alamy Stock Photo:** age fotostock (t). **Dreamstime.com:** Denis Kelly (bc); Ovydyborets (Background). **57 Alamy Stock Photo:** Hi-Story (tr). Dreamstime.com: Mikocreative67 (bl). **58 Dorling Kindersley:** Wallace Collection, London (cr). **Dreamstime.com:** Tomas Marek (clb). **iStockphoto.com:** thyme (br). **59 Dreamstime.com:** Nebojsa Mededovic (tl). **61 Alamy Stock Photo:** North Wind Picture Archives (tr). **64 Dreamstime.com:** Minnystock (tl)

**Endpaper images:** *Front:* **Alamy Stock Photo:** age fotostock crb; **Dorling Kindersley:** The Combined Military Services Museum (CMSM) br, Wallace Collection, London tr, cra; **Dreamstime.com:** Viacheslav Baranov bc; *Back:* **123RF.com:** Martin Hatch c; **Alamy Stock Photo:** Ionut David bc, Granger Historical Picture Archive tc, The History Collection cb, www.BibleLandPictures.com fcla; **Dreamstime.com:** Leonid Andronov fcr, Davidmartyn fbl, Dinosmichail cl, Speedfighter17 cr; **Getty Images:** Essam Al-Sudani / AFP fclb, DigitalGlobe fbr.

All other images © Dorling Kindersley
For further information see:
www.dkimages.com

## My Findout facts:

# Timeline of the castle age

Follow the timeline to find out about important events in the history of castles.

## Walls of Jericho
A defensive stone wall is built around Jericho in what is now Palestine.

## Walled city
Huge walls are built around Constantinople. The walls include walkways, tower forts, gatehouses, and moats.

## Stone castles
Motte-and-bailey castles are rebuilt with stone keeps and walls. These castles are built all over Europe.

Orford castle stone keep

## Bigger castles
Castles grow bigger, with round towers and multiple defenses.

| 8000 BCE | 2700 BCE | 270–400 CE | 300–400 | 900 | 1000–1100 | 1095–1291 | 1200 |
|---|---|---|---|---|---|---|---|

## City of Uruk
Massive stone walls, gatehouses, and a moat surround the ancient Iraqi city of Uruk.

## First castles
Castle building in northern Europe begins. Early castles had mottes and baileys, defended by ditches and fences.

Motte

Bailey

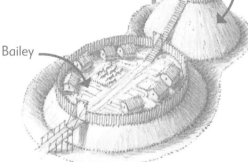

Ruins of Roman Burgh Castle

## Early forts
Romans build stone forts to defend English Channel coasts. Later, some were made into castles.

## Wars of religion
Crusades are fought between Christians and Muslims across Western Asia and Europe.

The Siege of Acre, in what is now Israel, lasted from 1189 to 1191.